The Great Unravelling

~

Why Democracy Failed, and How to Fix It.

An Essay by Julius Ruechel

*To the shining 'City on the Hill',
in the hope that it may be renewed
to inspire us all once again.*

Table of Contents

Introduction

"The countries concerned were compelled to abandon their tried and proven system, and replace it with the Western democratic system. Everywhere it has been implemented it has resulted in disaster and the complete antithesis of what was anticipated. The result was one man, one vote — once."

— Ian Smith, the last prime minister of Rhodesia before it became Zimbabwe.

Universal suffrage and progressive governance (social engineering) were promoted as benevolent ways to create a fairer, more just, and kinder world. Like so many utopian fairytales designed to put an end to abusive systems of the past, these alleged solutions to the shortcomings of older hierarchical democratic systems seemed unquestionably sensible and profoundly moral — at least in theory.

Everyone gets a voice. And those in need are given a helping hand by a government that puts its thumb on the scales if and when the need arises. Anyone in polite society who failed to enthusiastically endorse these two noble-sounding ideas clearly lacked a brain and a heart. And so, the entire post-WWII democratic foundations of the Western world have been built on these two untouchable philosophical foundations. And, by hook or by crook, the moral West immediately set out to spread their modernizing democratic update to the rest of the world.

Some of the first signs that this updated version of democracy might not live up to expectations emerged in Africa. As Rhodesia's recalcitrant prime minister Ian Smith pointed out as he tried in vain to resist the West's "update" from spreading to his country, the rapid transition to the Western democratic system immediately and invariably led to authoritarian disasters wherever it was introduced.

Once Britain, the United States, and other Western countries adopted a policy of pressuring non-Western countries to replace their existing systems of governance with "modern, inclusive, progressive democratic systems" (in which the ballot box was suddenly thrown wide open to one and all), one country after another across the whole of the African continent was systematically plunged into a rapidly escalating spiral of violence and plunder as various communists and socialists used the ballot box to seize power, proclaim themselves as king in all but name, and then weaponized their democratic institutions in a ruthless effort to hold on to that power forever. It amounted to revolutionary regime change, facilitated by the ballot box, and was immediately followed by the entrenchment of a kleptocratic one-party state masquerading as a democracy.

The same pattern emerged wherever the update spread in Asia, in South America, in Latin America, in the Caribbean, and in the Middle East.

Advocates of Western-style democracy invariably blamed "corrupt and powerful strongmen" for taking advantage of the system and turning these nations into corrupt tyrannies. Yet upon closer inspection it becomes apparent that this repeating blueprint for disaster is not because bad actors hijacked an otherwise good system, but rather because the modern Western democratic system as a whole is fundamentally flawed because it creates perverse incentives that attract a multitude of self-serving opportunists to the halls of power while simultaneously corrupting large portions of the voting public who cheer their rise in exchange for bread and circuses, funded by plundering everyone else in society.

The strongmen and the sponges in all their various forms are the consequences, not the root cause of the broken system. The system itself creates an irresistible web of destructive incentives whenever earlier systems of democracy are "updated" with this intoxicating combination of universal suffrage and a mandate to pursue progressive social engineering agendas. Any system that combines vastly expanded regulatory powers and vastly expanded tax collection powers with a population that can use the ballot box to pressure that massive government machinery to start re-engineering society for their benefit is a disaster just waiting to happen. The rats will overrun that system as certainly as any rat is lured to a giant stinking brick of cheese.

Any system whose continuity depends on the moral decency of philosopher-kings to prevent it from being corrupted, exploited, and repurposed for personal gain is doomed from the start. Once you look past the noble intentions, Western-style democracy amounts to little more than a red carpet laid out for every parasite, con-man, thief, professional victim, and would-be robber baron to try to enrich themselves at society's expense, either by finding a way to place themselves on the throne or by playing elaborate theatrical games to manipulate whoever is on the throne to shovel money and opportunities their way. Unlimited government creates unlimited opportunities for those willing to game the system to their own advantage.

There is no law, no regulation, no moral principle, and no threat of punishment that can discourage a rat from finding a way to unlock access to the cheese. The only solution is not to dangle cheese in front of rats.

Because human nature is opportunistic to its core, any system of government that's introduced to society must remain strictly limited in size and scope to prevent *anyone* — philosopher-king or rat — from gaining the authority to start fiddling with the day-to-day lives of their citizens or picking their pockets through taxation. Even the US Founding Fathers understood this as they framed a constitution designed for a government with a very limited reach, but the lesson was not heeded by those who inherited it.

If some version of the same disastrous outcome keeps repeating itself again and again wherever modern, expansive, inclusive, progressive, Western-style democracy is introduced, at some point you have to stop blaming "bad actors" and face the fact that the system itself incentivizes all the wrong behaviours and all the wrong people, irrespective of the good intentions of its architects.

But as long as the regime-orchestrated violence, naked corruption, economic destruction, nepotism, relentless inflation, and the systematic fleecing of society that followed on the heels of any transition to Western-style governance seemed confined to non-Western nations, it was easy to maintain the illusion that the fault lay with bad actors within those systems, not with the system itself. But now that same broken system of incentives produced by the modern Western democratic system is unravelling the West itself. And it's not just happening in one Western country. It's happening to them all.

It's happening to big multicultural Western nations like the United States, to small ethnically and culturally uniform Western nations like Sweden, to Western nations with deep roots in democratic traditions like Britain, and to Western nations that were only recently freed from communist tyranny and who should know better and be able to see the writing on the wall, like the Baltic states or the former regions of East Germany. And yet, it's happening to all of them, all at the same time, because they all blinded themselves with their good intentions, succumbed to group think, and thus unleashed the same broken system of incentives onto their societies.

Until recently, the unravelling of the West happened slowly enough to be able to deny the fact that what happened in the span of only a few years in places like Africa is also unfolding in Western nations, albeit on a slower timescale. We've not been immune; we've just been moving at a slower speed towards a similar destination. Time has made the unravelling visible as the compounding of rot spreading through our institutions has reached the tipping point where everything begins to feed on itself. As things crumble around us, things are starting to look increasingly similar to what unfolded everywhere else that the modern Western democratic system was introduced.

But why did it all go so wrong?

Since Rhodesia became the unlikely battleground between a global whirlwind of forces trying to impose their Western "update" onto the rest of the world (for a wide range of motivations) and a controversial little country trying desperately to resist it, this is a good place to start our journey to understand the rotten heart of the modern Western democratic system...

Africa's Hard Lessons
About Modern Western Democracy

Ian Smith feared that a rapid transition to "one man, one vote" in Rhodesia, thrust onto a population mired in poverty and lacking both education and experience with Western democratic systems, would inevitably lead to dictatorship, financial collapse, and chaos. His fears were not theoretical. They were based on witnessing that exact process repeat itself in countless countries across Africa, including in Rhodesia's next-door neighbors like Zambia, Malawi, and Mozambique as they spiralled into corrupt dysfunctional tyranny, one after the other, in the immediate aftermath of their transition to inclusive Western-style democracy.

And that's precisely what also happened to his own country when Rhodesia finally capitulated to Western pressure to abruptly grant every single citizen equal and unrestricted access to the ballot box. One man, one vote. Just as Ian Smith had predicted, a free, fair, and transparent election under this new system only happened once.

Robert Mugabe, Zimbabwe's infamous dictator, won that fateful first election in 1980. He renamed Rhodesia as Zimbabwe and then immediately set about transforming it into a de-facto one-party state that continues even today under the rule of his successors. He built an unshakable coalition of loyal supporters (predominantly organized along tribal lines), whose loyalty was bought by money, resources, and land expropriated from his critics. Once he and his coalition of loyal supporters sunk their claws into Zimbabwe's institutions, the regime became impossible to dislodge.

Together, he and his supporters unleashed a combination of coercion, intimidation, violence, arson, murder, and even genocide (against the rival Ndebele tribe) against anyone, black or white, who stood in his way in order to consolidate his grip on power. Even running out of money didn't stop him. He simply printed more to keep the money flowing to his loyal supporters, leading to the world's first 100-Trillion-Dollar bank note, which soon wasn't even worth enough to buy a single loaf of bread. Democracy becomes a farce once it falls into the hands of those willing to use taxation and the printing press to buy the loyalty of a coalition of dependent supporters... more on that later when this article turns to the forces unravelling the West.

In the years leading up to that fateful vote, Ian Smith tried in vain to advocate for a slow cultural and political transition to universal suffrage to give Rhodesia's diverse, impoverished, and historically tribal society the time to acquire the necessary education, political experience, and economic foundations to resist the destructive incentives of Western democracy.

Smith believed that any democratic system of governance cannot and will not survive for long without first doing the hard work of embedding classical liberal principles and values in the culture. By his estimation, culture provides the moral restraint to prevent democracy from spinning into a cycle of tyranny and exploitation.

In other words, democracy is as much a cultural system as it is a political system. As such, successfully introducing democracy to a society is much more complex than simply deciding, from one day to the next, to grant everyone equal access to the ballot box — a lesson the West has yet to learn as it turns one nation after another into an ash heap on its neo-con quest to impose Western-style democracy on the rest of the world.

But like in the rest of Africa, Soviet-trained and Western-backed nationalists in Rhodesia didn't want a gradual transition. They wanted an overnight revolution — and power — and so they played an effective game of leveraging their ever-expanding list of grievances to cultivate support from both Soviet and Western elites while using terror and murder as a tool to "incentivise" local tribal populations to jettison their traditional systems and jump on the democratic train. As Ian Smith once wrote about the tactics used by the guerillas terrorizing Rhodesia's tribal regions to "incentivize" them into supporting Mugabe and his peers, arson is a particularly evil weapon against a people living in wooden shacks with grass roofs.

Democracy. Now. For everyone. No compromises. Because that's the *moral* thing to do. Mugabe and his peers got what they wanted because the moral West felt compelled to take up their uncompromising "democratic" cause. In effect, Mugabe and his peers leveraged the West's own value system against them, weaponizing their empathy and their sense of morality for his own benefit.

The paternalistic West, catering to their own domestic political winds and under pressure from their media to "stand up for democracy", adopted a policy of appeasement towards Africa's communist and nationalist agitators. Thus, they pressured Ian Smith's government to abandon the idea of a *gradual* transition to universal suffrage — an idea that they themselves had pushed Smith to cement into Rhodesia's constitution only a few years earlier (to which he and the Rhodesian parliament had reluctantly agreed) in order to provide Rhodesia with a clearly defined pathway to transition away from the earlier principle of ballot access restricted by a property ownership and/or asset threshold. But now the idea of a gradual transition was no longer good enough. Now that too was scrapped and the transition had to be immediate, without any preconditions, and Rhodesia's parliament needed to get in line with this new moral target. Democracy now.

And so, the West forced Rhodesia to betray the very principle that it had itself pushed Rhodesia to write into its constitution to ensure that the transition would not throw Rhodesia into chaos. Instead, the West was now "all in" on Mugabe's bid for a revolutionary leap into instant all-inclusive "modern democracy", consequences be damned.

It's worth noting that Western countries had themselves only "updated" their own democracies a few years earlier to adopt this new principle of universal suffrage and to embrace this new idea of government taking a much more aggressive social engineering role in society — a process I wrote about in my recent book, *Plunderers of the Earth* (available on Amazon).

Prior to this modernizing "update", both Britain and America had political systems organized along the same principles as Rhodesia's system, with access to the ballot box requiring citizens to meet certain property ownership thresholds (unlike apartheid South Africa, ballot access in Rhodesia was never restricted by skin color, only by a strict property ownership threshold). Ironically, even today Canada still has an unelected Senate and the British Parliament still has an unelected House of Lords specifically to curb the heady appetites of the voting public. Do as I say, not as I do.

In other words, the "updates" to democracy demanded of others by these Western countries were still brand new and as yet unproven concepts even on their own soil. Yet, as soon as these countries made the decision to update their own democratic systems according to these new noble principles, they immediately set about using everything from crippling embargoes, trade sanctions, withdrawal of military support, and pressure through international organizations like the United Nations to make it mandatory for everyone else to immediately adopt the same one-size-fits-all system, irrespective of local circumstances. There is no end to the irony that America appointed itself as the world's moral policeman even as the ink was still wet on the civil rights acts repealing a century of Jim Crow laws in its own country.

Ian Smith was maligned throughout the West as a repugnant, unrepentant, bigoted, paternalistic, out-of-touch, self-serving racist and was turned into a villainous caricature in European and American pop culture, even as Mugabe was invited to give keynote speeches at UN climate conferences (and even appointed as a goodwill ambassador to the WHO) — and this was after Mugabe unleashed his genocide against the Ndebele tribe. Apparently western morality did have the flexibility to accommodate that.

Yet even after that fateful vote in 1980, Ian Smith's stature and popularity continued to grow inside Zimbabwe long after most white people had fled the country. As the Sunday Times reported in 2007, "*Africans of all persuasions flocked to Smith's house to consult him*)". He even received a standing ovation from the all-black student body at the University of Zimbabwe for a speech in which he fiercely condemned Mugabe's reign of terror.[1]

In 2002, Smith challenged Mugabe to join him for a joint walk through a black township, without security protection, to see which of the two men would get the best welcome '*Only one of us will come out alive*' Smith said; '*I'm ready to put that to the test right now. He's not.*'"[2,3] Mugabe did not take up the challenge.

---

[1] Johnson, RW. (2007, Nov 25). Lost paradise of the big white chief. *The Times.* https://www.thetimes.com/article/lost-paradise-of-the-big-white-chief-x0nzx93lf6r

[2] Johnson, R.W. (2007)

[3] "Ian Smith." *Wikipedia.* Retrieved 14 October 2024. https://en.wikipedia.org/wiki/Ian_Smith

Imposing Democracy on
Traditional Non-Western Cultures

Discussions about Rhodesia in Western media typically portray the Ian Smith era as a struggle by Rhodesia's white community to cling onto white rule. Reality is much more complex, with profound implications for us all even today as we watch Western democracy crumbling all around us.

There was much more at stake in Rhodesia than just its white-dominated parliamentary tradition (with ballot access determined by a property ownership threshold, not by skin color, though the only black Rhodesians who met that threshold were those living a modern Western lifestyle in the cities (and were indeed participating in the electoral process), whereas most of those living traditional lifestyles in communally-owned tribal lands did not the threshold).

What was also at stake were the traditional tribal systems of government that black Rhodesians had used for centuries to rule themselves, systems which at that time were still fully functioning in parallel with Rhodesia's parliamentary system.

Mugabe and his peers wanted to sweep both aside to get to universal *'one man, one vote'* democracy, which is why he terrorized the tribal lands and their leaders even more than he targeted Rhodesia's farmers in order to "incentivize" them to support his vision for Rhodesia, though we don't hear much about that part of the Bush War in Western media. In left-leaning Western media, Mugabe is typically portrayed as some kind of corrupted champion of African democracy, a "liberator" turned tyrant in the tradition of the fallen angel. The West's moral lens make many in the West incapable of seeing him as anything else.

BBC

Robert Mugabe: From liberator to tyrant

Robert Mugabe: From liberator to tyrant · Robert Gabriel Mugabe was a man who divided global public opinion like few others. · Zimbabwe's ex-...

Sep 6, 2019

Amnesty International Canada

Robert Mugabe: 1924-2019, a liberator turned oppressor

Robert Mugabe, who led Zimbabwe for almost four decades, has died aged 95, leaving behind an indelible stain on his country's human rights...

Sep 6, 2019

Washington Post

Opinion | Robert Mugabe was a liberator who turned into an oppressor. Zimbabweans remember both.

Opinion. Robert Mugabe was a liberator who turned into an oppressor. Zimbabweans remember both. · This praise may come as a surprise,...

Sep 7, 2019

Reuters

Zimbabwe's Mugabe: from liberator to oppressor

(Reuters) - Zimbabwe's Robert Mugabe was feted as an African liberation hero and champion of racial reconciliation when he first came to...

Sep 6, 2019

Another thing that the West attacked in its bid to help Mugabe and his peers bring "democracy" to Rhodesia was the fact that land in Rhodesia was divided into white and black areas outside of the cities. True liberation could only come about if this immoral relic of the colonial past was dismantled.

Once again, reality is a little more complicated, as Ian Smith himself tried to point out to the UK's prime minister Harold Wilson as the British dialed up pressure for Rhodesia to repeal the Land Apportionment Act during their negotiations over Rhodesian independence. An entire traditional tribal way of life was at risk, thrown into the negotiating pot by a shortsighted British government trying to score political points with its own British electorate earn the praise of its navel-gazing media, which had fallen under the spell cast by Mugabe and his peers. As we watch Wall Street and other foreign corporations gobble up land throughout our own Western countries, Ian Smith's words from his memoir, *Bitter Harvest: The Great Betrayal*, will have a familiar ring to them as an altogether different perspective comes into view:

> *"[...] were the British aware that if the [Land Apportionment] Act was repealed this would throw open the tribal trust lands to all races? These lands had from the beginning been reserved for the exclusive use of tribesmen, protecting them [and their way of life] from the big consortia, and the expertise, experience and finance of our white community. This would be absolutely catastrophic for our black people. There was a stony silence from the other side of the table. There were other examples of the dreadful ignorance of the British, which indicated all too plainly that they were not being guided by the interests of the country and its people, but were being motivated by political expediency, and a desire to meet the extravagant wishes of their friends, no matter what the cost."*

Rhodesia's struggle also became the focal point of the ideological clash happening throughout the West between a traditional classical liberal system based on the principle of limited government (and the conditions required to keep it limited, such as the property threshold to vote), and the new "updated" Western ideal of big, expansive, progressive, all-inclusive government — a difference as stark as comparing Thomas Jefferson's vision of limited government to Franklin D. Roosevelt's New Deal. Both go by the label of "democracy", yet they are entirely separate beasts.

In other words, boiling away inside the Rhodesia question were three entirely separate political systems (classical vs. "updated" democracy vs. traditional tribal systems of government. All three were colliding all at once in a perfect storm, with outside powers like Britain, America, and the Soviet Union using Rhodesia as a pawn both to further their games of international politics and to cater to their own domestic audiences.

Ian Smith wrote extensively about Rhodesia's traditional systems of tribal government, which continued to coexist in parallel with the parliamentary system, but which were at risk of being swept away by the sudden leap into the new Western democratic system:

"Their history, way of life and traditions were far removed from those of our Western civilization, and people of character and consequence do not lightly jettison their culture. Of course, there was no guarantee that we were right, and that they were wrong — time would tell and there was no need to rush these things. We were, after all, living in different worlds... "

He went on to write that:

"... [they] had their own traditional system which served them well. At the level of the extended family, or kraal, the leader emerged naturally through acceptance by the family, and, as long as he enjoyed their respect and confidence, he was their representative and spokesman. Whenever a problem arose which involved other kraals in their area, the kraalheads held a joint meeting. If the problem extended beyond their area of jurisdiction, they chose, from their midst, their representative, or Headman, to convey their message to their Chief, who was the leader of a much larger section of people. A Chief usually ruled the people of between four and six Headmen.

"Most problems were solved at that level, but if not, the Chief would take it to the next meeting of the Provincial Chiefs' Council (there were five provinces). Finally, there was the National Chiefs' Council.

"An analysis of the system points to many advantages. I know of no method which gives more honest and genuine representation, stemming from the 'grassroots' and ensuring

that the people's feelings are accurately submitted and explained. The system is devoid of corruption, nepotism, intimidation, propaganda and brainwashing, all those evil and undesirable ingredients which play such an important part in modern government.

"Those of us who live in sub-Saharan Africa and understand the traditions and customs of the people, have no option other than to condemn the actions of the major free world countries: in their typical arrogant manner, they took it upon themselves to lay down pre-conditions to the grant of independence. The countries concerned were compelled to abandon their tried and proven system, and replace it with the Western democratic system. Everywhere it has been implemented it has resulted in disaster and the complete antithesis of what was anticipated. The result was one man one vote — once.

"Today sub-Saharan Africa is riddled by one-party dictatorships or military dictatorships, financially bankrupt and in chaos. If only people would come and see for themselves — I have yet to find a single fair-minded person who has not been convinced after a visit. It is easy, when you live ten thousand kilometers away, to prescribe solutions, knowing that if the whole thing blows up and goes sour, you do not have to live with the results.

"The finest guarantee that the rest of the world can have, that we are completely dedicated to producing the best solution for all of our people, whatever their race, colour or creed, is that we, and our children after us, will have to go on living with the result..."

As an aside, it is worth noting that one of the reasons the traditional tribal system described by Ian Smith worked so well is that it involved neither taxation or redistribution nor anyone with the authority to impose social engineering endeavours on everyone else — it worked precisely because no-one could use their authority to plunder anyone else or impose their ideas on anyone else. It was a system for resolving conflicts, not for tax collecting or social engineering.

Smith understood the different worlds that needed to come together under a single umbrella, the risks and incentives created by the Western system, and the difficult cultural transition required to bring them together. The West did not.

The Incentives Create the Culture

Although Ian Smith clearly foresaw what would follow in the aftermath of the revolutionary leap into Western-style democracy, I have come to firmly disagree with his belief that time, culture, and a gradual transition could have bridged the gap and prevented some version of what ultimately unfolded after Rhodesia's revolutionary leap into wholesale modern Western-style democracy.

Time itself has passed judgement on the "updated" Western democratic system, not just in Zimbabwe but also in the countries of the West itself — the well-spring of classical liberal culture — where that same updated democratic system is likewise now in terminal collapse. Culture wasn't enough to prevent an unravelling even among nations with centuries of cultural immersion in classical liberal principles and values, which have simply melted away before the caustic incentives created by the updated system.

So, I think it is fair to say that Ian Smith's belief that culture could restrain the ruinous incentives created by the modern Western-style democratic system if Rhodesia's transition from tribal to modern democracy had unfolded slowly enough was just as unrealistic as everyone else's belief that instant universal access to the ballot box was the righteous and moral path towards a better future. Whether by revolutionary leap or gradual transition, the modern version of Western democracy was doomed in Rhodesia just as it is failing in the West itself. Ian Smith's struggle was an unwinnable battle to hold back a tide.

In fairness to Smith, the modern "updated" democratic system was pushed onto him. It's only through pressure from the West that 'one man, one vote' ever became the official end-goal for Rhodesia's gradual transition. Before the West got involved to push their preferred vision onto Rhodesia, his conscience and his initial goal had been to build a bridge from the tribal system to Rhodesia's older parliamentary tradition, not to modern "updated" democracy in which every single citizen has unrestricted access to the ballot box.

Would Rhodesia have continued to be prosperous and peaceful if the older parliamentary tradition had remained as the end-goal of Rhodesia's gradual transition? Perhaps if the rest of the world had also continued living under that older system, in time he might have successfully bridged the divide between the two parallel worlds co-existing within Rhodesia's borders as ever greater numbers of black Rhodesians transitioned from a traditional tribal lifestyle to participating in the modern free market economy.

But I suspect that once the rest of world embraced the idea of universal suffrage as the new moral standard for democracy and turned its back on the earlier system as an abusive relic of the past, the die was cast. No-one would have been content to settle for anything less than 'one man, one vote', and every single conflict, grievance, and wealth disparity in the country would have forever been bitterly interpreted through the lens of Rhodesia hanging on to a relic form of democracy from the past — that too would have been a recipe for the country to ultimately tear itself apart.

In a globalized world of television, radio, and internet, no country can persist as an island — the spread of ideas in a globalized world adds a new dimension to the political arena that makes it very difficult for any country to march according to the beat of its own drum without being pulled into the orbit of ideas that are in vogue among its neighbors. In the end, Rhodesia imploded not because of pressures arising from within Rhodesia itself but because of the pressures imported into the country by Marxist-trained Mugabe and his ilk. Mugabe himself describe his student years at the University of Fort Hare in South Africa, where he was exposed to Marxism, as the "turning point" in his life that completely reshaped the lens through which he viewed the world.

Short of building a wall to keep outside ideas out and citizens trapped within to prevent them from being "corrupted" by ideas circulating outside of the country's borders (as modelled by North Korea or China's Great Firewall of internet censorship), for better or for worse no modern country participating in the global economy can prevent its citizens from being influenced by ideas circulating outside its borders.

As long as the end-goals of Western democracy continue to be defined as universal suffrage combined with a masterful administrative state empowered to pursue social engineering agendas — the lethal one-two punch of modern Western-style democracy — whether you leap in by democratic revolution, or slowly grow your way in over time, once any country "updates" itself with these new ideas, the perverse incentives created by these two pillars of modern Western-style democracy will invariably eat away at the foundations of the culture. Culture merely determines the speed of the unravelling, but it cannot change the direction of travel created by the destructive incentives of this updated system.

In short, the die was cast on the day that the West as a whole turned its back on the classical liberal principles of limited government and embraced this new vision for a fairer, more just, kinder, and more inclusive world.

All the education, economic development, and cultural development in the world cannot compensate for a system that incentivizes voters to use the ballot box to gain a parasitic advantage for themselves while incentivizing politicians to use the public purse and the legislative pen to leverage taxes and regulation to purchase the loyalty of a coalition of dependant supporters.

Once social engineering (and the taxation that enables it) becomes an accepted part of the role that government is expected to play, and once the beneficiaries of those social engineering efforts acquire a taste for government money and learn to leverage the power of the ballot box as a means to support their parasitic way of life, these "pillars of modern democracy" become wrecking balls that unravel any society that adopts them. For example, there's nothing mysterious about the rise of victimhood culture in all its bizarre ever-changing forms — at its heart, it's nothing more than the product of the incentives created by social engineering and affirmative action policies.

Earlier democratic systems undoubtedly left many people without a voice, especially in Western countries that no longer had functioning parallel traditional systems of government like those still functioning in tribal areas of Rhodesia during the Ian Smith era. Earlier democratic systems also undoubtedly allowed those with access to the ballot box — particularly those who lacked the moral fortitude of philosopher-kings — to use their ballot, influence, and political donations to stack the system in their favor.

But that doesn't automatically mean that granting everyone equal access to the ballot box or that expanding the government's ability to tax, spend, and put its thumb on the scales will produce better results — on the contrary, now there's simply a different and much bigger rotten game afoot with a different set of winners and losers. And government has become an even more attractive magnet for everyone with dreams of power and plunder.

The unravelling that has invariably followed the transition to a "kinder, fairer, more inclusive" version of democracy makes it very clear that, however much the previous system needed updating, the updates provided by modern Western democracy have proved toxic to any society that adopts them. Yet another utopian fantasy is revealed to be nothing more than fairytales and pixie dust because the design of the system itself (and thus the incentives created by that system) are completely out of touch with the opportunistic reality of human nature.

From our vantage point today, we can see that *no* culture has been able to resist the destructive incentives created by the modern "updated" version of Western democracy. Furthermore, it's not just that culture failed to hold back corrupt incentives, it's that it doesn't take long for these incentives to completely reshape and re-write the culture itself.

The rise of victimhood culture, climate hysteria, the pronoun wars, and a never-ending, ever-expanding list of other bizarre parasitic beliefs that have taken root in our culture are all byproducts of a culture responding to the incentives created by the modern democratic system. If you can get enough people to start voting according to those beliefs, your "tribe" can gain sympathy, power, opportunities, and preferential treatment under the current system. The very thought that not every problem should be the government's responsibility to solve is enough to get you thrown out of polite society these days — culture has adapted to the incentives.

The system creates the incentives, and the incentives create the culture. All the other rot emerges downstream from there.

The West's Greasy Slide into Suffocating Bureaucratic Tyranny

The leap from functioning system to tyrannical one-party state was completed in the course of a single election cycle in Rhodesia. In Western countries that transition has taken much longer. But the re-written culture that emerged on the heels of the "update" to modern Western democracy is now dissolving all the classical liberal cultural restraints that once kept our own democratic systems from unravelling into the extreme levels of chaos, oppression, and tyranny witnessed under Africa's strongmen. What is emerging in the West isn't identical, but it increasingly rhymes.

Our system is now also growing increasingly authoritarian fangs and claws and accelerating the speed at which it bleeds its own people through taxation, inflation, and so on. Our own system is also becoming increasingly aggressive in the game of using taxes and regulation to buy the loyalty of regime supporters with bread and circuses at the expense of everyone else. And our regimes are increasingly turning to age-old tricks to silence, censor, disappear, or assassinate anyone they don't like. The law is whatever the regime wants it to be and applies only to those that the regime wants it to apply to.

Only in our version, what has evolved over time is not a leap into kleptocratic strongman rule, but rather a kind of slow greasy slide into kleptocratic bureaucratic strangulation facilitated by an emergent increasingly aggressive transnational one-party quasi-corporate Deep State that disguises itself with democratic theatrics.

~

The failure of Western-style democratic systems in non-Western countries is often partially blamed on their tribal culture, whereas democracy was allegedly successful in the West because Western culture had supposedly long-since moved beyond tribal identities and tribal ways of thinking about politics. And yet, in addition to the cycle of naked corruption, economic destruction, inflation, exploitation, and growing regime-orchestrated violence and oppression that is emerging in Western countries, the incentives of Western-style democracy are also fueling the re-emergence of increasingly intolerant tribal ways of thinking throughout the supposedly enlightened liberal West. Except, in the West these emergent tribal divisions are not rooted in traditional tribal cultural identities but are being invented (and re-invented), day by day, to suit whatever narratives are useful in the never-ending game to curry favor with the regime in exchange for favors.

It turns out that tribalism is not merely a cultural phenomenon rooted in language and religion, it is also something that can be created spontaneously, purely as a consequence of incentives that reward tribal behaviour. In other words, if you update your democratic system to turn it into a political machine that enables exploitation, persecution, and the redistribution of resources from one group to another, militant tribalism spontaneously re-emerges from those incentives.

Your political affiliation, your religious beliefs, your victimhood identity, your skin color, your gender, your sexual orientation, your pronoun, and even the vehicle you drive and the way you cut or dye your hair have all become increasingly potent tribal markers as Western democracy turns tribal. If Western democracy is capable of producing tribalism even in a culture that previously wasn't tribal, then Africa's failure to create successful Western-style democratic utopias cannot be blamed on Africa's tribal traditions.

On the contrary — in reality it was the overlay of Western-style democracy onto tribal culture that was responsible for highlighting and intensifying those tribal divisions as the incentives of the ballot box fueled opportunities to rally together as a tribe to plunder other tribes through the stroke of the regulator's pen or through the power of the tax collector, while simultaneously motivating everyone else to take refuge in their tribal identity in an effort to shield themselves from being plundered by others. A tax-and-spend democracy is the perfect crucible for putting tribalism on steroids.

Rhodesia's tribal system in the pre-modern democratic era, as described by Ian Smith earlier in this article, was the opposite — it lacked the corruption, intimidation, nepotism, propaganda, and brainwashing that we typically associate with tribalism because, until it was overlain by the tax-and-spend economy of the Western democratic system, there were no incentives to fuel these destructive outcomes.

Tribalism undeniably has its own problems and is certainly responsible for shedding a lot of blood across history as rival tribes competed for territory. But in the modern African story, it is the overlay of the Western democratic system onto tribal culture, not tribalism itself, that is to blame for the spiral into tribal violence, bloodshed, and exploitation along tribal lines after these nations were "liberated" by democracy, only to find themselves competing for the spoils of taxation, regulation, and centralized control.

In order for any modern democratic system of government to be judged as a success, that system must succeed in defusing society's tribal tensions, not reinforce them, in order to prevent society from tearing itself apart. And it most certainly should not produce tribalism where it previously didn't exist. Modern Western democracy is an absolute failure on both counts.

With each passing day, it becomes ever more apparent that we are on the same ruinous path taken by our African peers as our cultures respond to the same incentives created by our democratic systems. It's just that African nations (like so many other countries across the world) were plunged into the modern Western democratic system by a single revolutionary coup carried out via the ballot box, whereas the West was spared the sudden revolution only to end up in the same place by evolution as the earlier culture gradually gave way to the same incentives.

And whereas these other countries already had pre-existing tribal divisions that immediately flared into violence as soon as they were exposed to the incentives of the modern Western democratic system, in the West it has taken a little longer to build those tribal divisions from scratch — but we're getting there nonetheless. In other words, we're all moving towards the same destination, albeit at different speeds.

What's Behind the Curtain, Grand Conspiracies or Perverse Incentives?

It has become very popular in some circles to blame every twist and turn of the unravelling currently happening in the West on grand conspiracies operating in the background. While it is true that there are a lot of what I would call *lesser conspiracies* trying to game the system in their favor, these conspirators are little more than well-positioned parasites positioning themselves to feed on the incentives of a rotting system. You could round up all of these conspirators, lock them in a dungeon, and throw away the key, but the incentives of the system would remain intact.

One crop of conspirators would quickly be replaced by another, just as one deposed African dictator is soon followed by another, and just as one rat will soon be followed by another if you leave food laying out to attract them on the kitchen floor. These lesser conspirators are not the architects of the unravelling, they are merely responding to the incentives of the system in the same way that a rat follows its nose to the cheese. The conspiracies will continue, indefinitely, until you take away the cheese.

If you're looking for grand conspiracies, you'd be better off looking back to the likes of Woodrow Wilson, Franklin D. Roosevelt, Vladmir Lenin, Joseph Stalin, and all their contemporaries in the era when these ideas first came into vogue. These are the men who conspired to build the political architectures to translate new ideas about democracy, government responsibilities, and economic systems into actual government systems, and then adopted the policies to spread these beliefs and these systems to the rest of the world.

They "updated" the system to turn trendy new ideas about liberalism, socialism, communism, and fascism into actual government systems. They set the system of incentives in motion;

everything else flows from there. If we're going to stop the unravelling, the culture war from which a new vision can emerge must begin by recognizing the source and the bankruptcy of those ideas.

But the most ominous realization that emerges when we view the unravelling of the Western democratic system is to recognize the trajectory of the unravelling. So many other non-Western countries have already trodden this path in earlier decades. Their outcomes were not pretty. With such an intoxicating amount of virtually unlimited power concentrated in the hands of our leaders, along with the combined incentives of wanting to hold onto that power, the blind tribal loyalties that emerge as political tribes compete for the throne, the systematic "othering" of competing tribes, and the ruthless persecution of would-be reformers who threaten to upset their ill-begotten empire, this combination of incentives ultimately deteriorated into horrific levels of violence, censorship, oppression, civil war, and even genocide.

Western-style democracy isn't just some stable boiling pot of never-ending petty corruption and oppression. As the perverse incentives continue to eat away at society's foundations, all too frequently that boiling pot has boiled over into horrors that are, as yet, unimaginable to Western citizens who have not seen those things on their own soil in a century or more. A quiet century has bred complacency and a dangerous resistance to reform because "those terrible things can't happen here in our culture".

We haven't reached tinpot-dictator-levels of violence. Yet. But the growing tribalism, the growing impoverishment of the once-productive parts of society who are now being systematically plundered and left behind by the system, the othering, the continuing decay of the justice system into a system of arbitrarily enforced laws, and the increasing use of vindictive lawfare by the regime against dissenting voices are all deeply troubling indications of the dangerous trajectory we are on.

What begins as voters exploiting the ballot box as a means to empower government to act as Robin Hood on their behalf all too often accelerates into a spiral of violence at the hands of an entrenched regime as it seeks to defend its hold on increasingly dictatorial power and as it builds a system (often along tribal lines) designed to systematically plunder some groups to buy the loyalty of others.

In short, the day we created a Robin Hood redistribution system, we began the process of fracturing our society into warring tribes, fighting to decide who benefits and who gets plundered.

Modern Western democracy isn't a stable system — it is self-radicalizing as those who acquire a taste for power and taxpayer money go to increasingly extreme lengths to defend their way of life. And the coalition of loyal supporters who feel entitled to share in the spoils of the regime's plunder is willing to support and even participate in ever more extreme forms of persecution in order to preserve their way of life. Modern Western democracy ultimately incentivizes the emergence of a morality fit for thieves, parasites, and tyrants. As we saw during Covid, empathy for the "other" is rapidly evaporating as neighbor turns against neighbor along newly forming tribal lines. Covid was a window into similar feelings boiling away beneath the surface of our culture along so many other new tribal divisions emerging in our culture.

Cover of the August 26th, 2021 edition of the Toronto Star

The Blandest Tyranny in History

Modern democracy, with its vastly expanded powers of taxation and regulation, is the ideal vehicle with which to build loyal coalitions of dependant supporters. Welfare systems, government contracts, subsidies, research grants, regulatory advantages, affirmative action policies, legal protections (i.e. liability waivers for pharma), immigration promises, and countless other politically controlled "things" are all levers that buy political loyalty in a system in which voters and their donors can use the political process to stack the deck in their favor.

It happens automatically as the incentives ensure that these never-ending programs perpetually grow ever larger, but the most successful politicians and parties are those who learn the art of ruthlessly leveraging these tools to build an unshakable base of loyal voters at the polls. And it doesn't happen in a vacuum — as it gets normalized, it begins to reshape culture itself and fuel expectations for more.

For example, one of the key architects of America's vastly expanded bureaucratic state, President Franklin D. Roosevelt, was notorious for his willingness to leverage taxpayer money and regulation to play favorites, and to stack institutions with those who shared his socialist beliefs. The imprint he left on our institutions, voter attitudes, and party strategies continues to haunt us to this day.

Once a vote is bought, it is bought for however long the flow of money and opportunities continue to flow. If you wonder why there are so many destructive, wasteful, and senseless programs that just never seem to get repealed — such as corn ethanol subsidies, the Jones Act that gives U.S.-flagged ships a monopoly on transporting cargo between the mainland and Puerto Rico, the U.S. sugar subsidies for U.S. sugar producers, government housing projects that cost taxpayers multiple times more than if those buildings were built by private industry, and the list goes on and on — each micro-tribe of beneficiaries represents a tiny slice of the coalition, which would howl like their life depends on it if anyone tried to fiddle with the program. Keeping them quiet and loyal by keeping the gravy train intact keeps everybody happy, and taxpayers won't even notice what it is that they're funding.

And since paying for this ever-expanding gravy train isn't going to be popular with taxpayers (and since everyone continually wants more of it for their own benefit), everything gets funded with more debt, followed by the printing press to inflate away those debts, which fuels a persistent inflation that robs taxpayers by stealth because inflation doesn't require passing laws in order to pick the pockets of the taxpayer. Those inflation targets are then sold to the public as "good for the economy" while anyone who disagrees is accused of being "irresponsible" and "economically illiterate."

The incentives for everyone — politician, donor, and voter alike — favor keeping the merry-go-round spinning, no matter the cost to the future, so everyone can keep getting their goodies today. It's a broken system… and almost everyone has an incentive to keep it that way.

At more than $35 Trillion in government debt (that's more than $100,000 debt, before interest, for every single man, woman, and child alive in America today), the problem looming in the background is so colossal that it's pretty much career suicide for any politician to do anything about it — the entire West has essentially locked itself into a slow suicidal cycle of debt and inflation, like virtually every empire that has come and gone before it.

As prosperity is inflated away, wealth slowly accumulates in the hands of the asset-holders who benefit from inflation, while hollowing out everyone else. The day Wilson, Roosevelt, and their compatriots set the West onto a path of government managed, taxpayer funded social engineering for the "collective good", the die was cast for the gradual hollowing out of… well, everything.

The idea that a shoe salesman will be able to afford to raise a family and expect to own a single-family home on a single income, like he once could expect in the 1960s, is a fantasy relic of the past, slowly and silently destroyed by the destructive spiral of public debt and inflation. Mugabe's printing press just killed the Zimbabwean dream faster.

Any politician or party who can piece together a broad enough coalition of these well-rewarded "micro-tribes" using the many levers at their disposal becomes impervious to scandal, can say just about any stupid thing you can imagine without affecting their poll numbers, and pretty much run the rest of the country into a ditch without consequences to their chances for re-election. Society's best and brightest are essentially squeezed out of the political system as the grease floats to the top of the modern democratic system, and stays there, held in place by their loyal coalition of loyal dependants.

One of the great enduring myths about democracy is that elections are about policies, principles, and values — a wise and principled people stepping back every four years to consider what's best for their country as their leaders presenting them with competing visions for their nation's future. It's a beautiful fiction. In reality, everything that politicians say and do is about signaling which groups will be rewarded and which will be plundered during their reign. And some voter groups are more susceptible to being bought than others by virtue of their circumstances or by virtue of their character — the least moral and most selfish members of society become the most reliable members of the coalition. Modern democracy is the perfect vehicle with which to hold civilization hostage to the worse aspects of human nature.

"Government is the great fiction though which everybody endeavors to live at the expense of everybody else."

— Frederic Bastiat.

The reason leftist politicians are so successful at getting re-elected despite the never-ending stream of nonsense coming out of their mouths is that they have no qualms about deliberately plundering the most productive members of society to buy the loyalty of a broad coalition of dependent supporters using the power of the public purse and the regulator's pen. It's not quite as blatant as Mugabe's antics in Zimbabwe — more of a Mugabe-lite — but it's the same idea and continually grows worse over time.

And all the rhetoric circulating around society helps convince the beneficiaries of this broken system that they are rightfully entitled to their stream of benefits. Those who receive a gift from Robin Hood don't have to think about who that "gift" actually comes from, how it fell into the hands of Robin Hood in the first place, and how much better off everyone would be and how much healthier the culture as a whole would be if Robin Hood wasn't constantly robbing everyone for someone else's benefit in the first place.

Those who come to depend on the government in some way or another will remain loyal supporters of whichever leader or party is most likely to preserve their government-dependent way of life — no-one votes to burn the bridge they are standing on. And so, the trajectory of decline is locked in.

To take Canada as an example, 44% of the money spent inside the country is spent directly by the government. If you factor in compliance costs, the impact of tax subsidies on spending priorities, and the coercive effects of regulation, that number rises to 64%, as calculated by the Macdonald-Laurier Institute.[1]

This is a massive gravy train.

No political party can make any meaningful reform to such a system because if they do, they will upset all the beneficiaries of this gravy train and automatically lose at the polls, which is why their rhetoric may differ but there is remarkable continuity between their governing policies no matter who gets elected.

---

[1] "Size of government in Canada." *Macdonald-Laurier Institute*. Accessed 12 Oct 2024. https://macdonaldlaurier.ca/size-of-government-in-canada/

With such a colossal tax-and-spend system, beneficiaries have gained so much power at the polls just by virtue of their numbers that Canada's entire democratic system of government is essentially at the mercy of keeping everyone who benefits from that gravy train happy.

Politicians can try to gain new supporters by adding yet more programs to cater to additional special interest groups, but they can't dismantle anything without upsetting the applecart. And so, the system becomes a one-way ratchet towards ever greater taxation, ever greater regulation, and ever greater social engineering schemes to keep the beneficiaries of the system happy, while the productive members of society must bear an ever-growing burden to keep the government's gravy train flowing smoothly. And you're permanently propagandized to convince you of the morality and necessity of accepting that ever-growing burden.

The bigger the system gets, the more people figure out how to take advantage of it to make sure that as much gravy as possible ends up in their pockets. You don't need a strongman at the top to end up with a system strangling itself with corruption and exploitation, you merely need a never-ending stream of feckless self-serving politicians continually catering to special interest groups to making Leviathan ever larger. When's the last time you saw government dismantle anything? As the saying goes, *there's nothing more permanent than a temporary government program.*

Equally ominous is the expanding size of the government itself. 1 in 4 employed Canadians now works directly for one of the various branches of government (federal, provincial, and municipal, and the myriad of bureaucratic institutions that make them function).[2] Now consider that during elections, only around 60% of eligible voters bother to vote. Yet almost every public sector employee is likely to vote — they're even given paid time off to go do so — which means

---

[2] "A Quarter of Employed Canadians Now Work For The Government." (2024, Aug 9). *Better Dwelling.* https://betterdwelling.com/a-quarter-of-employed-canadians-now-work-for-the-government/

that the 25% of Canadians who work in the public sector actually represent closer to 42% of the voters who bother to vote.

In other words, *Canadians whose salaries depend directly on the government are thus the single largest voting block in Canadian elections.* The net result is that expansive Western-style democracy incentivizes government to view its primary purpose as doing whatever it takes to keep its own government employees happy.

In short, government is being run for the benefit of those who work for the government.

Factor in everyone whose business depends on government contracts or subsidies, anyone whose business is dependent on regulatory advantages provided by the current government, anyone who digs ditches, builds roads, or provides services for the government, and anyone who collects welfare or benefits from some government program, and you quickly understand why an entrenched regime reaches a point, even without strongman rule, where it is nearly impossible to dislodge or reform no matter how corrupt, tyrannical, and predatory it becomes towards everyone who is not a part of that coalition of core loyal dependants.

And so, the incentives of the system drive the system to ever more perverse extremes.

The conflict of interest created by universal access to the ballot box is obvious. In a sane world, no-one who is a net beneficiary of government money, whether through direct salaries, contracts, social programs, grants, or subsidies should have been eligible to vote. It was fine while government was small and before society embraced the tax-and-spend philosophy of widespread social engineering. It stopped being fine as soon as modern Western democracy was updated with these dangerous new incentives.

The moment that any coalition of government dependants is given access to the ballot box, their conflict of interest inevitably ensures that big government ceases to be the servant of the people and becomes instead the servant of its coalition of dependants... and the master to everyone else. But good luck rolling back this little oversight...

And so, we find ourselves in the bizarre situation in which, by virtue of this obvious unresolved conflict of interest, government's primary purpose is now to serve itself. Not necessarily because there's some Mugabe-style strongman in charge or some Illuminati working behind the scenes with a carefully crafted master plan, but simply because the government is its own biggest and most dependable and most motivated voting block. It is, quite literally, the blandest tyranny in history.

The ballooning growth of this system also fuels its radicalization. The bigger the system gets, the more opportunities for corruption, and thus the greater the incentives to weaponize the bureaucratic tools of the state to censor, silence, and punish anyone trying to bring accountability to the out-of-control system. Being a whistleblower has become a life-threatening choice. Just ask Edward Snowden. Or Julian Assange.

And the continual growth of taxation ensures that the productive members of society have to be squeezed harder and harder, fueling unrest as they reach the limits of what they can bear. It's a recipe for an increasingly paranoid and authoritarian state.

Those who have come to depend on the regime and feel entitled to their slice of this ill-begotten pie won't bat an eye as the regime does whatever is necessary to keep them happy and keep the flow of money and privileges flowing. The system's extreme immune reaction to President Trump's declaration that he intends to "drain the swamp" has been revealing of the true nature of what lies beneath the surface of the modern democratic system as all the various factions that are somehow beneficiaries of the entrenched regime rally together to fend of this threat to their way of life.

~

Ian Smith was wrong in his assumption that culture would be sufficient to hold back the destructive incentives of modern democracy. He recognized the vulnerability of Zimbabwe's tribal culture to the effects of Western democracy, but he did not recognize that his own British culture was equally at risk of being torn apart by the incentives of Western democracy, albeit on a slower timescale.

He continually expressed his frustration and bewilderment during his negotiations with the British and the Americans that they had seemingly all gone mad and abandoned all principles and foresight in how they approached the Rhodesia question. What he failed to recognize was that their madness was itself the effect of the destructive incentives of modern "updated" Western democracy as those incentives handicapped their own ability to make sensible political decisions. Many of these same leaders agreed with Smith in private and even told him so, as he reports in his memoirs, and yet they simultaneously refused to change course in public as they continued to cater to voter opinion in their home countries, leading them to continually ramp up the pressure on Rhodesia when it came time for policy to be put to paper in front of the eyes of the world.

That's yet another lesson in this tragic story: While government business that's allowed to be conducted behind sealed doors leads to rampant corruption, as soon as democracy became a public, transparent process conducted in full view of the world, it turned into a public spectacle as everyone gets caught up in the game of catering to fickle public opinions and fickle public fits of outrage as they play to their respective audiences. If you read about the history of the French Revolution, one of the catalysts that drove things to reach the extremes of guillotines in the streets was that, for the first time in French history, political debates began to be conducted in public, in front of live audiences, instead of in cloistered chambers. Everyone began to play to their supporters in the crowd, rather than genuinely debating any of the real issues at hand.

Radio, television, internet, and social media have had a similar effect. Everything is about soundbites and viewership ratings. The bigger that we allowed government to get, the more issues are of public interest, the bigger the audience gets, and the more that heated emotional audiences drive political decisions.

The only solution is to keep government as small as possible to limit the scope and reach of the spectacle. Instead of deluding ourselves that politicians can resist playing to the spectacle as fickle audiences watch from the sidelines and as media fuels outrage to drive ratings, we have to redesign the system to democratic system to defuse the spectacle — the only way to do that is to keep the government as small as possible with a mandate to defend our rights and not much else.

If you watch Trump's rise, he is almost entirely a creation of the media putting a permanent spotlight on him and continually telling the world that he is an existential threat to civilization. The media has leveraged outrage against him into a spectacularly successful strategy to save their collapsing industry. Trump drives ratings. And if the unhinged hysteria that the media has fueled in half of the population leads the country into civil war, so much the better for the flailing media — viewership scores would be off the charts.

Ian Smith wrote about how he felt deeply betrayed by the West. Earlier in life he had emphatically declared that he (like most white Rhodesians) was culturally "more British than the British themselves." Yet during his negotiations for Rhodesian independence, he found himself standing up for long-established Western democratic principles that Britain itself was now flushing down the toilet.

By the time the failed negotiations effectively delivered Rhodesia to Mugabe and his radical peers on a silver platter, Ian Smith's view of himself had completely changed. As Wikipedia reports, in a 2005 interview Smith asserted that he viewed himself as African, stating "*I was born here. My children were born here, and my grandchildren were born here. I'm African, not British.*"[3] Although he never took the official step of renouncing his dual British citizenship, he ceased

---

[3] "Ian Smith." *Wikipedia.* Retrieved 14 October 2024.
   https://en.wikipedia.org/wiki/Ian_Smith

renewing his British passport and, many years later, when Zimbabwe stripped him of his citizenship in a tightening of Zimbabwe's citizenship laws, Smith announced he was now stateless. Ultimately, Zimbabwe allowed him to remain in the country but refused to renew his passport.

It is telling that Ian Smith chose to remain in Zimbabwe after Mugabe rose to power despite the clear risks to his life and property instead of choosing to flee to safety in the West. Zimbabwe was home whereas the West had become foreign as its decaying culture evolved according to the incentives of the new "modern" democratic era. And it was the West and Western culture that had betrayed him and the vision he had for his beloved country.

The West went back to their distant lives ten thousand kilometers away after the whole thing went sour following Mugabe's rise to power. Yet, even as most of the remaining white Rhodesians fled for their lives, Ian Smith stayed in Zimbabwe for the rest of his life. After his death in 2007, his farm, like so many other farms before his, was finally seized by Mugabe's regime as part of yet another wave of Mugabe's land reform programme.

And perhaps that's the final lesson in this tragic story: as we moved from classical liberal democracy to modern Western democracy, there has been an accompanying shift of decision-making away from locals (who ultimately have to live with the consequences of the political decisions that affect their lives). Instead, by virtue of the evolving democratic system towards an ever more "optimized", centralized, and bureaucratized system, decision-making authority has been transferred into the hands of ever more distant decision-makers and into the hands of voters in far-off places. In effect, local voters are completely outnumbered and shut out of the decisions that affect their lives

None of these distant decision-makers — distant voters and politicians alike — have any real stake in the outcome. They pay no price for being wrong and never have to live with any of the day-to-day realities of what their decisions create, and yet their opinion matters infinitely more in the decision-making process than the small number of locals who ultimately have to live with each decision that is made.

As decision-making has increasingly shifted from the kraal, farm, and local community to provincial and federal parliaments, to nameless and faceless bureaucrats working in distant bureaucracies that have to craft one-size-fits all solutions for entire countries, and to "experts" working in distant and unaccountable transnational institutions, those who have no skin in the game get to make all the decisions and those who have no voice in the decision-making process get to pick up the tab.

This shift of decision-making responsibility into ever more distant hands is perhaps the single-most destructive force of all tearing democracy apart in the West. Everyone is responsible for everyone else and is empowered to stick their noses into everyone else's affairs, yet no-one is allowed to be fully responsible for themselves anymore.

And that, in a nutshell, is a look into the history and future trajectory of modern, inclusive, progressive Western-style democracy.

What Comes After Democracy?

When the Roman Republic reached this dysfunctional juncture in the evolution of its civilization, it put a stop to the unravelling by turning to dictatorship and then imperial rule. The transition from republic to empire was marked by a bitter civil war to decide the first ruler of this new imperial era. Augustus won the civil war and is considered the second founder of Rome because of his benevolent rule in the tradition of a philosopher-king, which breathed new life into Rome.

But a mere three generations after Augustus, his tyrannical great-grandson Caligula is rumored to have appointed his horse to the Senate in a spiteful move designed to humiliate the senators and show them how irrelevant they had become within the imperial system. Caligula's reign of terror came to an early end when he was murdered by a conspiracy of officers of the Praetorian Guard collaborating with senators and courtiers. The transfer of power is the Achilles Heel of monarchy and dictatorship. If only they had found a way to revive their republic instead.

Once a rotting democratic system reaches this point in its evolution, it becomes increasingly tempting to reach for strongman rule as an escape from broken democracy. The people themselves begin to crave it in order to find relief from an increasingly dysfunctional and predatory democratic system. But even if you're fortunate enough to get a philosopher-king in the first round, who inherits his throne? Because in the line of succession, every Augustus will eventually be followed by a Caligula, a Nero, and a Commodus. Who will rule over your children and grandchildren? How do you prevent a system of strongmen from merely re-creating the same trajectory into self-serving madness, corruption, inflation, nepotism, exploitation, and war? No emperor rules alone — he too needs a coalition of loyal supporters. And they too will demand favors, money, and opportunities in exchange for their loyalty.

If we're going to fix the broken incentives of Western-style democracy without giving up on the benefits of democracy itself, we're going to have to face up to the reality that the "updates" that were made to Western democracy during the late 19th and the first half of the 20th century put Western Civilization on a path to self-destruction. The prior system was undeniably full of flaws and hypocrisies that urgently needed fixing. What we have now is even worse.

If we're going to give every single citizen equal and unrestricted access to the ballot box, we cannot also give the government the authority to engage in social engineering. These two things are not compatible. No nation, no culture, no society can survive the incentives of this lethal combination without ultimately tearing itself apart.

If we're going to open the ballot box to everyone, we must limit government authority to the narrowly restricted role of defending individual rights... and not much else. Otherwise, the voting mob (and more accurately, those who learn to manipulate the voting mob with propaganda, coercion, terror, or money) will inevitably turn the democratic system into Hell.

Alternately, if we're going to give government a mandate to engage in social engineering for the alleged benefit of the greater good, we better suspend democracy first and make sure we find a philosopher-king to rule us to prevent self-serving voters from turning social engineering into a never-ending game to stack the deck in their favor. And no-one gets to complain if the chosen philosopher-king doesn't pursue *their* preferred vision of how society should be "engineered". One man's Augustus is another's Caligula — the dividing line of opinion typically depends on whether the gravy train flows towards or away from you. After all, someone has to pay for it all. And brace for the fact that even if the philosopher-king does happen to give you what you want, no-one rules forever. The difference between living under Augustus versus Caligula is only a matter of time.

No matter how you look at it, social engineering is a terrible update, irregardless of who is in charge of it. Leviathan has to be shrunk to a mere fraction of its current size so that neither philosopher-kings nor rats have any real power if they ascend to the throne.

Furthermore, although it may already be a criminal sin to say this out loud considering the touchstone that 'one man, one vote' has become in modern culture, but universal suffrage urgently needs some limits placed upon it in order to counteract the most obvious conflict of interest in our democratic system. Ballot access *must* be denied to anyone who is a net beneficiary of government spending (not for life, but for as long as someone receives taxpayer money, subsidies, contracts, or favors from the government). And the vote most especially must be denied to anyone who works for government for as long as they receive a salary paid by taxpayers. Public service should be a noble and respected sacrifice, but the servant of the people cannot be allowed to simultaneously be their master. It's simply not possible to stop the expansion of government as long as this conflict of interest persists.

The evolution of society must be allowed to take its own organic course, not be directed by the prodding of central planners. And as much decision-making power as possible should be transferred back into local hands — those who must live with the consequences of those decisions. It would also help greatly to split provinces into smaller micro-provinces, and especially for large cities to automatically become their own city-provinces, similar to cities like Hamburg or Bremen in Germany, where the municipal and provincial boundaries are one and the same. The city saves itself the cost and complication of an entire extra layer of government and the cost of carrying poorer rural areas, and the rural areas are spared the burden of city voters deciding how country people should live their life. Win-win.

The federal layer of government is thus reduced to defending borders and defending citizens rights and liberties from encroachment by local and provincial governments — all other decisions are pushed down to a more local level.

Of course, as social engineering retreats, local communities, the private sector, private charities, and volunteer efforts have to step in to fill the void, just as they once did before we rolled out the modern, progressive, centrally-directed welfare state. This, in turn, will help revive a culture in which local reputations matter, which revives honesty and integrity within communities. The incentives shape the culture. At its core, like so much of what shapes the world, morality is a product of incentives.

The solutions are not easy. Don't expect the bloated regime and its coalition of dependants to go quietly into that goodnight. There are few red lines that a cornered rat will not cross to preserve itself and its way of life — the more it feels threatened, the more paranoid and vicious it will become.

Convincing the people that democracy itself needs to be changed, rather than just the people running it, might prove to be the biggest hurdle of all. Buying loyalty with bread and circuses is easy. Taking them away again... not so much.

We live at the crossroads of very different possible futures depending on how all this plays out.

~

"The hardest lesson of my life has come to me late. It is that a nation can win its freedom without its people becoming free."

— Joshua Nkomo, Mugabe's former co-conspirator during the Bush War years, and later second vice-president of Zimbabwe, before he was forced to flee Zimbabwe when Mugabe launched the Gukurahundi genocide against his tribe.

About the Author

Julius Ruechel has a BSc of Geology from the University of Alaska, Fairbanks. He is the author of:

- *Grass-Fed Cattle: How to Produce and Market Natural Beef* (a how-to guide for farmers based on his experiences in the cattle industry),
- *Autopsy of a Pandemic: The Lies, the Gamble, and the Covid-Zero Con* (an investigation into the government's mishandling of the Covid pandemic), and
- *Plunderers of the Earth: the Erosion of Civilization, the Mad Crusade to Control the Climate, and the Untold Stories of Soil and CO$_2$* (a deep dive into how political and ecological systems unravel — often in tandem).

You can read more of his essays and explore his independent investigative journalism on his website at *www.juliusruechel.com*. And you can read his articles about raising cattle on his educational cattle farming website at *www.grass-fed-solutions.com*.

9 798344 217345